STOP CHASING, START CREATING

STOP CHASING, START CREATING

A Timeless Fable on Mindset, Resilience, and Meaningful Work

JUSTIN JONES-FOSU

Berrett-Koehler Publishers

Berrett-Koehler Publishers, Inc.
1333 Broadway, Suite P100
Oakland, CA 94612-1921
(510) 817-2277
bkconnection.com

Ordering Information
Quantity sales. Special discounts are available on quantity purchases by corporations, associations, individuals, and others. For details, please go to bkconnection.com to see our bulk discounts or contact bookorders@bkpub.com for more information.
Textbook exam/desk copies. Please consult the General FAQ at bkconnection.com.
Bookstore orders for trade or textbook use. For print books, please contact Penguin Random House Publisher Services at customerservice@penguinrandomhouse.com. For ebooks, contact your favorite distributor.

Distributed to the US trade and internationally by Penguin Random House Publisher Services.

The authorized representative in the EU for product safety and compliance is EU Compliance Partner, Pärnu mnt. 139b-14, 11317 Tallinn, Estonia, www.eucompliancepartner.com, +372 5368 65 02.

Printed in the United States of America

Berrett-Koehler books are printed on long-lasting acid-free paper. When it is available, we choose paper that has been manufactured by environmentally responsible processes. These may include using trees grown in sustainable forests, incorporating recycled paper, minimizing chlorine in bleaching, or recycling the energy produced at the paper mill.

Library of Congress Cataloging-in-Publication Data
Names: Jones-Fosu, Justin author
Title: Stop chasing, start creating : a timeless fable on mindset, resilience, and meaningful work / Justin Jones-Fosu.
Description: Oakland, CA : Berrett-Koehler Publishers, [2026]
Identifiers: LCCN 2025046753 (print) | LCCN 2025046754 (ebook) | ISBN 9798890572141 paperback | ISBN 9798890572158 pdf | ISBN 9798890572165 epub
Subjects: LCSH: Job satisfaction | Employee motivation | Self-realization
Classification: LCC HF5549.5.J63 J62955 2026 (print) | LCC HF5549.5.J63 (ebook) | DDC 650.1—dc23/eng/20260316
LC record available at https://lccn.loc.gov/2025046753
LC ebook record available at https://lccn.loc.gov/2025046754

First Edition
35 34 33 32 31 30 29 28 27 26 10 9 8 7 6 5 4 3 2 1

Book production: Westchester Publishing Services
Cover design: Ashley Ingram
Cover and interior art: Heelmonster Studio

To my mother—**Mom-e**—

Thank you for teaching me the power of Creating. For showing me, not through speeches, but through daily rhythms, that the internal aspects of life—the character, the courage, the clarity—are so much more valuable than the external ones.

You reminded me that what I create on the inside will always outlast what others see outside.

This book is rooted in your wisdom.

With love and deep gratitude,

Your Justy-poo
Justin

CONTENTS

AN INVITATION TO THE JOURNEY

Dear Reader,

You don't need another book telling you to run harder or do more.

You need space to remember why you started running in the first place—and to ask whether you're even in the right race.

Stop Chasing, Start Creating isn't a roadmap—it's a rhythm.
It's a story about finding alignment in a world that rewards busyness,
about choosing purpose over performance,
and about rediscovering what truly matters in the work you do and the life you lead.

If you're reading or listening to this book,
there's a good chance you've been running—
maybe not on a track,
but through the quiet noise of deadlines, expectations,
and the constant need to prove that what you do *matters.*

Perhaps you've built a good life and still feel a tug that something's missing.
Maybe you've been chasing success, approval, or recognition—only to find that the finish line keeps moving.

I know that feeling.
I've lived it.

I wrote this book for you.

For the leader whose calendar is full but whose heart feels somewhat empty.
For the professional who keeps achieving but still wonders, *Is this it?*
For the parent, partner, or dreamer who wants to create a life that feels aligned—not just impressive.
For anyone who's tired of chasing what fades and ready to create what lasts.

This book was born from a personal realization:
I had been living like the Hare—in constant motion, productive, busy, and applauded—
yet increasingly disconnected from meaning.

It wasn't speed that was the problem; it was direction.
I was moving quickly, but not meaningfully.

When I began creating from alignment instead of chasing applause,
everything started to shift.

That shift marked the beginning of what I now call my **Tortoise Journey**—
a journey of learning to work, lead, and live from the inside out.

But let me be clear: I haven't arrived.
I still wrestle with the pull to perform, prove, and please.
Some days, the chase still calls my name.
The difference now is that I hear it—and choose differently, even if imperfectly.

This book isn't written from a place of arrival.
It's written from the middle—
from the tension between who I was and who I'm becoming.

What started as reflection has become a rhythm,
one I'm still learning to walk every day.

In a world overflowing with content and information,
what we don't need now is more noise.

What we need is a way to learn differently—
to feel differently—
so that we can embrace the right content at the right time.

That's why this book is a fable.
Facts inform the mind,
but stories shape the heart.

We don't just remember lessons;
we remember the characters who lived them,
the choices they wrestled with,
and the truths they discovered along the way.

The story you're about to embark on is not just about a tortoise named Tano—
it's about all of us.

It's about the moments we quit when no one's watching,
the voices that drive our pace,

and the courage it takes to create something meaningful in a world that celebrates speed.

The book unfolds in three parts:

- **The Story**—a fable to feel and reflect on.
- **The Practice**—tools and reflections to help you live the story.
- **The Resources**—next steps to help you lead and share the message with others.

Each part is designed to meet you where you are—
whether you're reading on your own,
with a team,
or inside an organization that's ready to reimagine what meaningful work looks like.

My hope is simple:
that as you walk this story, you'll rediscover your rhythm.
I hope you'll find the courage to stop chasing, start creating, and build a life aligned with what truly matters.

Because when you stop chasing what fades,
you start creating what lasts.

So as you turn the page into Tano's journey, don't just read it.
Walk it.
Feel it.
Let it ask you questions you didn't know you needed to answer.

Because in a culture of chasing,
the courage to create may be the most needed wisdom of all.

And so, our story begins . . .

—Justin Jones-Fosu

THE STORY

THE STORY BEFORE THE STORY

"Dadda, were you always that brave?"

The question stopped him more abruptly than any finish line ever had.

For Tano the day had been long but meaningful at Forest International, an organization strengthening what most creatures never saw—building systems that kept the forest healthy, resilient, and able to grow without losing its roots. But when Tano, the tortoise, stepped into his children's room, the weight of decisions and deadlines gave way to the softer rhythm of bedtime. He tucked in the twins, answered his oldest child's last-minute question, and sat by his baby girl, who never fell asleep without one more story. "People always tell us about the race you won against the Hare," she whispered. "Were you always that brave to race a fast Hare like that?" The other three peeked out from under their blankets, waiting.

Tano smiled gently. "Let me tell you how the story is usually told first." He retold the old fable—the Hare darting ahead, the Tortoise plodding on, the Hare's nap, and the Tortoise's quiet victory. The familiar moral was this: ***slow and steady wins the race.***

When he finished, his daughter frowned. "But was the race really like that?"

Tano nodded thoughtfully. "Not exactly. The world liked to call me slow—because that's what they saw when they compared me to the Hare. But I was never slow. I was steady. And steady was enough." He paused, his voice softening as the room grew still. "The truth is, before that day, I wasn't always steady either. I was chasing something else. Applause. Attention. The kind of validation that doesn't last." He leaned closer, lowering his voice like he was sharing a secret. "If you want the real story, we have to go back—long before the starting line."

The children's eyes widened. Even the twins, who were halfway asleep, each opened one eye.

Tano chuckled softly. "This isn't the story they tell in classrooms," he said. "This one doesn't start with a race. It starts with a restlessness—the first chase none of us realizes we've begun." He looked toward the window of the children's room, where the moonlight stretched across the floor like a trail. "Before I ever stood on that starting line, I had to face another kind of race—the one inside myself."

He glanced back at them, the smallest smile forming beneath the weight of memory. "So if you really want to know how it all began ..." He exhaled slowly, eyes distant. "You'll have to walk with me—back to the days when my shell felt heavier than my hope, and before I ever learned that steady could be strong." He paused, then whispered almost to himself: "Because the story before the story... was the one that changed everything."

As Tano reflected about his thoughts from that first race, he didn't know then that everything he'd ever chased was about to be tested—and that the first thing he'd lose was himself.

ALMOST SAID

Chapter 1

THE SHELL THAT WEIGHED TOO MUCH

Before the race, there was restlessness.

Tano had learned early that silence drew less ridicule—but it had also stolen his voice. Every morning at Forest International, Tano polished his shell until it gleamed. He checked his presentation slides twice, rehearsed his talking points, and entered the building looking like a tortoise who had it all together. Reliable. Professional. The one everyone could count on.

And that was the problem.

He had become the dependable one—the shell everyone leaned on, but no one celebrated. The steady worker. The safe pair of hands. The one who made things run but never made things shine.

It wasn't the first time he'd felt unseen.

As a young tortoise, Tano learned early that silence drew less ridicule. His shell had been a favorite target for teasing—too thick, too dull, and it slowed him down. The other young ones mocked him for the way he thought before he spoke, for how he paused to understand before responding.

His father left when Tano was still small, promising to come back "when things settled." They never did. What settled instead was a quiet belief that maybe Tano wasn't worth staying for. His mother did her best, but absence has a way of echoing louder than presence.

So, he worked harder. He spoke less. He tried to prove through performance what he feared he lacked in worth. Every polished shell, every perfect slide, and every late-night rehearsal was a quiet attempt to earn the "I see you" he'd never heard.

At night, he told himself it was enough—that being dependable was noble, even meaningful. But every award ceremony, every email blast praising someone else's "innovation" left a small crack in that belief. He wanted to clap for others, he truly did—but a quieter voice inside always whispered, ***"When will it be me?"***

There was a part of him that wanted more than to be steady. He wanted to be seen. Not out of arrogance, but out of hunger—for someone to look past the reliability and recognize the soul behind it. To say his work mattered. That he mattered.

People liked him. But no one really saw him.

In meetings, he had unspoken insights sharpened like stones struck for fire. But he waited. And he waited again. And by the time he spoke, someone else—usually Harold—had already filled the silence.

Harold, the Hare in every way that mattered, didn't even need to try. He spoke first, spoke fast, and somehow spoke in a way that made people laugh, nod, and lean forward.

The irony was sharp: the more careful Tano became, the more invisible he felt.

Sometimes, late after work at his work desk, he wrote in a notebook section he'd created titled **Almost Said**—a private record of everything he swallowed instead of speaking.

- *Almost said:* "That strategy is all flash, no foundation."
- *Almost said:* "We're confusing speed with direction."
- *Almost said:* "I respectfully disagree."
- *Almost said:* "If one more person says 'synergy' before lunch, my shell might crack."

Page after page filled with brilliance no one heard. The meeting notes never reflected Tano's unspoken contributions.

Forest International rewarded visibility. Promotions went to the bold employees. The spotlight favored the loudest ones. And though Tano's work was steady and reliable, steady and reliable didn't trend on the intranet.

At night, he replayed conversations, adjusting words that were never spoken. He stayed up repolishing slides no one would remember, because they never remembered what Tano presented in the past. The shell on his back wasn't just bone—it was the weight of proving his worth through visible success.

Some nights, his spouse, Ama, would wait up for him, half-asleep on the couch, the TV still murmuring in the background. He'd promise, ***"Just one more edit,"*** but ***one more*** edit of his slides always turned into two.

Their marriage wasn't unraveling from fights, but from absence dressed up as ambition. With every chase for recognition at work, he drifted further from the home where appreciation waited without conditions.

He'd watch others rise, their names mentioned in meetings or spotlighted in company updates, while his name stayed buried in places no one really read or cared about. It wasn't jealousy—it was ache. He wanted to believe steady mattered, but steady rarely made headlines.

His spouse finally said what he couldn't. "You're not working for impact anymore," said Ama, "You're working for applause."

Tano tried to laugh it off. "Well, if they gave trophies for pixel-perfect slides, I'd have a wing in the trophy hall." But the joke didn't lift the ache. He knew Ama was right.

Because what he craved wasn't the work itself.

It was being seen.

When the email arrived announcing the **Trailblazer Race**—an event designed to find "the next face of leadership"—his pulse quickened. The race involved a short presentation, a cross-department challenge, a team project, and an endurance course. Visibility guaranteed.

His computer cursor hovered over **Apply**. He closed the window. He opened it again. The cursor blinked like it was daring him. ***"Maybe this is how I finally matter,"*** he thought.

He clicked.

The confirmation email came before his self-doubt could undo the application he just submitted.

At lunch, he told a teammate casually, as though the decision were no big deal. "I think I'm signing up for the Trailblazer Race. Figured it's time to stretch myself."
The teammate raised an eyebrow. "Didn't you say you were done with the visibility game?"

Tano shrugged. "Maybe I'm just tired of not being seen." He smiled as if it were a joke. But deep inside, it wasn't.

Because beneath the polished shell, one truth had been shaping him all along:

He wasn't creating impact.

He was chasing validation.

And the chase was wearing him down.

He didn't know it yet, but the next email he opened would decide whether the chase consumed him—or finally cracked his shell.

Chapter 2

THE ACHE TO BE SEEN

The Trailblazer Race confirmation email blinked in his inbox like a spotlight he couldn't ignore.

Congratulations—you're officially in.

Tano's shell tingled with both thrill and dread. This was the moment. He could finally be seen. He opened his slide deck. Version three took shape by lunch. By dinner, he was on version six. By version fourteen, he wondered if the slides he was preparing even mattered.

Each revision pushed the words further away from who he was. They started to sound less like him and more like the kind of lines people clap for. The applause in his head was louder than the voice in his chest. And he wondered, when the applause stopped, would there be anything left of his voice at all?

Across the cafeteria, Harold—the Hare in every possible sense—was already working the room. He balanced a tray on one knee while cracking a joke that had the table laughing loud enough for the orb camera, a small hovering lens that tracked attention, to tilt toward him. He didn't announce he was in the race. He implied it with ease. Everyone believed him.

Tano watched, gut heavy. ***Why is it so effortless for him? Why do I need twelve versions to feel legitimate?***

Near the back wall, Petra from HR warmed her tea in the microwave. Everyone called her the "HR badger"—patient, steady, quietly watching over almost everything while the louder creatures darted through the halls. She smiled easily, but her eyes carried the tired kindness of someone who had once run too hard for someone else's approval. Tano barely noticed how often she'd covered for others or diffused small conflicts before they grew bigger.

Petra wasn't one for small talk, but there was a steadiness in her presence that felt earned. The kind of steadiness that only came from falling apart once and deciding to rebuild slower. Maybe that was why she noticed people like Tano—the ones trying too hard not to disappear.

She walked over to Tano's table. "How's the prep?" she asked, mug steaming.

"Solid," he said automatically.

"You always do solid," she said. "But don't forget to breathe."

He forced a chuckle. "I'll pencil it in between versions fifteen and sixteen."

But he didn't breathe. He kept chasing. Because the ache to be seen wasn't about ambition. It was about invisibility. Being reliable meant being forgettable, and he knew it. And that ache clung to him more heavily than any shell. He thought the ache would fade once the race began. Instead, it grew stronger.

He thought the ache would fade once the race began. Instead, it grew stronger.

Chapter 3

THE HIDDEN BURDEN OF THE STARTING LINE

The day of the presentations arrived with more buzz than a hornet's nest in spring.

Forest International shimmered with energy—but for Tano, it felt more like exposure than excitement. Leaf-backed chairs filled the central grove, banners shouted ***Rise and Lead,*** and the orb camera—a floating drone lens that streamed every moment—hovered above the grove, capturing every nervous and shining smile.

Tano's name was fourth in the presentation lineup. He held his notes, though he didn't need them. When the orb camera zoomed in, he delivered every practiced line with calm precision. Purpose. Alignment. Then a safe joke about tortoises and gym memberships—how he always brought his own resistance, in the form of a shell.

The applause was polite. Professional. And quickly forgotten. Polite applause was its own kind of silence. For a moment, he stood in that quiet, realizing this was what he'd been chasing—the sound of approval that faded before it reached his ears. It should have felt like progress, but it only felt hollow. All the effort, all the polish, and still . . . it wasn't enough to fill the ache to be seen, to be acknowledged, to be applauded.

Then Harold bounded forward, empty-handed, no slides, no notes. He told a story about growing up with six siblings, learning to be quick just to get dinner. He moved with rhythm, improvised with ease, and had the crowd laughing before his second sentence.

The orb camera hovered closer, almost as if it were entertained. Tano wondered if technology itself had favorites. For a moment, Tano wondered if even all the animals of the forest leaned toward Harold's voice.

He folded his notes tighter. He didn't need to hear the ending. He already knew the outcome: Harold wasn't just in the race. Harold was the race.

He didn't envy Harold's charisma. He envied how Harold never had to ask, ***Am I enough?*** The crowd answered it for him every time.

Later that afternoon, the final phase was announced: a one-day endurance challenge through the forest perimeter. Tano's chest tightened. Another chance to prove he mattered. Another stage where applause might finally find him.

But even as Harold's earlier ovation echoed in his mind, Tano sensed the forest had other plans—this race would test more than his legs. It would test his motives, his rhythm, and whether what he was seeking mattered at all.

Polite applause was its own kind of silence.

FINISH

Chapter 4

THE MOMENT HE STEPPED OFF

The morning of the endurance challenge dawned with skies too cheerful for what the day demanded. The orb camera hovered above the starting line, quietly tracking faces as contestants stretched and smiled for it—performing confidence they hadn't yet earned.

Harold trotted over, exuding charisma and proving the rules of sweat didn't apply to him. "You're steady, Tano. I admire that. Tell you what—" he clapped Tano's shell with a grin wide enough for the orb camera to catch—"I'll give you a head start."

The laughter from the group wasn't cruel. But it wasn't kind either.

The whistle blew.

Tano moved with intention. Breath. Step. Breath. Step. He moved with intention, neither hurried nor hesitant. He knew his rhythm. At the first marker, he felt strong. At the second, he believed he might even belong.

Then came Harold. The Hare didn't run past—he glided. He winked at the orb camera as if it were his personal fan club. The crowd watching online would remember Harold's laugh more than Tano's sweat.

By mile three, Tano stumbled. Not from exhaustion—his legs still had more to give. He stumbled under the weight of comparison pressing down on his shell. The orb camera hovered ahead, chasing Harold's highlight reel. Tano felt the sting of being left behind when he yearned to be in front and heralded like Harold.

By mile four, he stopped. He sank onto a moss-covered rock just off the trail. The truth was harsher than the heat: he hadn't stepped off because his body gave out. He stepped off because his identity was tethered to winning. And if he couldn't win, he believed he wasn't enough.

The orb camera drifted on, pulled toward Harold and the promise of a highlight reel. Tano stayed where he was until the trail emptied and the forest reclaimed its silence. He didn't announce his exit. He waited for the noise to move on, then took the long way back—each step slower than the last, not from fatigue, but from the weight of what he was carrying. By the time he reached home, the day had already folded in on itself.

That night, Tano sat on the porch, staring into the dark. Ama, his loving wife, found him there.

"You okay?" she asked.

Tano hesitated. "I thought I had something to prove," he said. "Turns out, I was just tired of not being seen."

Ama sat beside him. "We see you. Even when you don't."

He hadn't meant to drift away from her. He had never thought of himself as absent. But chasing didn't always look like running—it often looked like staying late, proving his worth to people who barely knew him, and returning home to the quiet of someone who had already believed in him.

He was only beginning to understand it now: the chase carried a cost. And too often, it was paid by the people closest to him.

A message blinked across his computer screen in the quiet of his home office.

Petra: When are you coming back to work?

Tano: I don't think I'm built for this.

Petra: You are. Just not in the way you thought. And I'm proud of the work you did to prepare for the race.

Tano: Is it ok if I take a few days away from work?

Petra: Absolutely. I am here if you need a listening ear.

Her words didn't erase the shame of not finishing. But they cut through the silence with something steadier: being seen. And as the room settled back into quiet, Tano felt a question surface that he had spent years outrunning.

If he wasn't the racer...
If he wasn't the achiever...
If he wasn't the dependable one...

Then who was he?

Chapter 5

THE LETTER AND THE LEGACY

The question followed him into the morning. He didn't return to the trail. He didn't return to work. And he didn't return to the version of himself that had always known what to do next.

Instead, Tano walked deeper into the forest, not in search of answers but away from the life that no longer fit. With each step, something familiar loosened as he grew closer and closer to his late grandmother's cottage.

His steps slowed as he neared a clearing that smelled faintly of barkroot tea and memory. The old home came into view. The door creaked when he pushed it open, as if surprised it had a visitor.

Inside, dust clung to every surface, but warmth lingered. Shelves bowed with worn books, his grandmother's chair still by the window. He sank onto her reading bench, the same one where she had read to him as a child. For the first time in days, he let himself be still. That's when he noticed it: a floorboard slightly raised.

Carefully, he pried it loose. Beneath it lay a bundle wrapped in vine-thread and faded fabric. He lifted it carefully and unwrapped it. It was a scroll; its bark handles carved with care. The parchment was uneven, the ink bled and was smudged, and there were tea rings circling corners. It was not polished but was well worn.

Across the first page, faint words: **The Creating Rhythm: 67 Wise Sayings to Shape a Shell from the Inside Out.**

Tano tilted his head. Sixty-seven? Oddly specific. Then he had a revelation: a tortoise's shell wasn't one piece. Dozens of bones fused together to form strength.

He unrolled the scroll carefully, letting his eyes wander across the faded ink. He didn't stop at every line—just the ones that seemed to reach out and whisper to him.

#7—*Meaning begins in small acts that outlive you.*

The words tugged at him. He thought of moments he had dismissed as too small to matter—a kind word, an unseen effort, the mentoring conversations that no orb camera would ever capture.

His eyes drifted further.

#29—*Curiosity makes your world larger than your fears.*

He exhaled, remembering the times he had shut down, protecting himself with silence, when curiosity might have opened the door instead. Further still, another line seemed to glow on the parchment:

#40—*Confidence doesn't come from applause. It comes from alignment.*

He swallowed hard. The truth of the statement landed with weight. Applause had been his fuel, but it burned out too quickly. Alignment—with his values, his pace, his purpose—was something he had barely begun to understand. Then, near the end of the scroll, his eyes landed on the final number.

#67.

He looked at it once. Then again. And again. What he saw settled deep within him, dislodging something he hadn't known was stuck. He couldn't explain why, but he knew this much: #67 would change him forever.

His mind raced as he noticed a brittle note tucked between the folds, written in his grandmother's careful hand. He unfolded it slowly.

Tano, my precious boy,

I have watched you—even now—chasing after so many things, hoping they would make you feel whole. But the chase never delivers—only leaves you emptier, hungrier, and more exhausted than before. And yet so often, when you did catch them, you were too worn out to enjoy them. Other times, what you caught didn't feel the way you thought it would. And sometimes what you chased just kept moving, always staying ahead, as you compared yourself again and again.

Do you see it, Tano? The chase will never give you what you are looking for. It only leaves you emptier, hungrier, and more exhausted than before. I want more for you. I want you to live free of the endless race that steals your joy and blinds you to your worth.

I spent years chasing too—thinking if I worked hard enough, they'd finally clap. Sometimes they did. But it never filled me.

So hear me clearly: Stop chasing. Start creating.

When you stop chasing applause, titles, and comparisons, you will finally have the energy to create what matters—alignment, rhythm, and resilience. That is where meaningful work and a meaningful life are found. That is the legacy I hope you will carry.

And, Tano, this wisdom isn't only for you. Every tortoise, every hare, every creature in the forest needs it. Because we all chase things that will never fill us. You are not alone in this.

My hope, Tano, is that one day you will no longer chase what fades but create what lasts. That you will walk steady—in alignment, in rhythm, in resilience. Because when you do, you'll finally discover the truth: this is your race, your pace.

He shook as he lowered the letter. The words felt heavier than the parchment in his lap. He pressed the note to his shell, tears warming the edges of his eyes. For the first time, he admitted what he had refused to say aloud: ***She was right. This is me.***

He had chased. And chased. And chased. He had caught things only to find them hollow. He had reached milestones

but felt invisible. He had compared his pace until he could barely breathe.
And now, in this quiet cottage, he realized the words were not just for him. They were for anyone who had ever grown tired of the chase.

He closed the scroll, his heart pounding. "I want to stop chasing," he whispered. "I want to start creating." A pause. "But . . . what now?"

He had no idea. But for the first time in a long time, not knowing didn't feel like failure. It felt like possibility.

Still, one number on that scroll he couldn't get off of his mind: #67. What could it mean—for his work, his life, and something more he couldn't yet name?

MASTERY
MOMENTUM
MINDSET
THE MEANING JOURNEY MODEL

Chapter 6

BECOMING WITHOUT PROVING

Three days later, Tano returned to Forest International with the scroll still tucked in his bag. He hadn't told anyone about it—not the sayings, not his grandmother's letter, not #67. It felt too heavy, too personal, too alive to share. He still didn't understand the full weight of #67—but somehow, it was already rewriting him.

But the words kept circling him, echoing in the quiet: ***Stop chasing. Start creating.*** The possibility of it all lingered for days, heavy and unresolved. And just when he wondered where to begin creating, there was a knock on his office door. "Mind if I come in?" Petra asked, balancing her mug that read *Practice Grace.*

Tano gestured toward the chair. "Sure."

Tano looked up from his desk as Petra stepped in—the same steady HR badger who'd been quietly rooting for him long before he realized he needed it. Her eyes fell on the edge of the scroll peeking from his bag. She paused, then smiled—a knowing curl of the mouth. "You found it."

Tano's head snapped up. "Wait—what do you mean ***found it***? You know about this?"

Petra nodded slowly. "Yes. Because your grandmother once mentored me." The words hit him harder than he expected. His grandmother had mentored her?

Petra leaned back, remembering. "I was younger then. Ambitious. Restless. Chasing everything. Titles, recognition, applause. She saw right through me. She let me borrow that scroll for a season. I tried to decode it like it was a puzzle, thought I could master it with my brain alone." She paused, tracing the rim of her mug. "The truth is ... I wasn't just chasing success. I was chasing someone too—my mother. She had this picture of who I should be—poised, perfect, never messy. Every promotion, every polished presentation was really for her. I thought if I performed well enough and had all the right titles and prestige, she might finally see me."

Her voice softened, the words fragile but sure. "When I finally stopped chasing her approval, I didn't feel free right away. I felt lost. Because chasing had been my rhythm for so long. But your grandmother helped me see that the ache wasn't failure—it was space. Space to start creating something new. Not to impress, but to align."

Tano stayed quiet, letting the words land.

"Your grandmother saw through that mask faster than anyone ever had," Petra said, her voice low but steady. "She told me I was chasing for a woman who might never clap—and that I had to stop renting my worth from her approval, living as though my value expired the moment the applause stopped."

She exhaled, a faint smile tugging at the corner of her mouth. "That's when I started to create instead of chase. Not all at once. But little by little, she taught me that peace is louder than perfection. Even now, I still catch myself polishing that same mask. Healing doesn't mean the ache disappears—it just means it doesn't drive you anymore." She gave a small, almost self-conscious laugh. "Some days, I still catch myself refreshing my inbox, waiting for someone to notice the things I swore I didn't need noticed." Her gaze drifted toward the window, her voice softening. "You learn to quiet the chase, but it never fully disappears."

Her eyes softened. "And then I reached #67. It unraveled me. I went back to her, expecting her to explain it. She just laughed that wise laugh of hers and said, 'You don't need to understand it yet. You need to walk it.'"

Tano sat, frozen. His grandmother had walked Petra through the very journey he was about to begin. Somehow, it felt like she was still mentoring him—just through Petra now.

Petra pulled out her notebook and drew a simple triangle (see figure 1). At each corner she wrote:

Mindset → Momentum → Mastery

Petra turned her notebook toward him. "Mindset, Momentum, Mastery." She tapped each corner of the triangle.

"That's a lot," Tano murmured, leaning in.

"It is," Petra nodded. "But it's not a checklist. It's a rhythm. She walked me through it one step at a time. And now, I think it's time she walks you through it—through me."

Tano studied the triangle. "Why counterclockwise?"

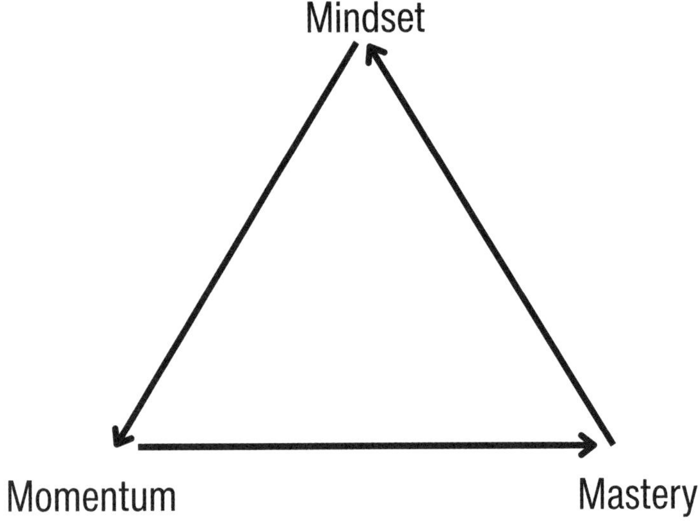

Figure 1. The Meaning Journey Model.

Petra smiled. "Everyone else runs clockwise—up and to the right. Bigger. Faster. Louder. But meaning doesn't always move that way. Sometimes, it takes you back. To what's wise. To what's true."

Tano gave a weary laugh. "So, growth feels like swimming against the current?"

"Exactly," Petra said. "Each stage showed up for me when I needed it most. Some months it was about shifting my mindset. Other times it was about building rhythms. Later, it was resilience when I faced doubt and silence." She paused, then smiled. "But don't worry about all of that now—we'll walk through each one when it's time. Your grandmother never rushed me, and I won't rush you." Tano shifted uncomfortably. "I don't know if I can do this with you. I don't like asking for help."

Petra raised an eyebrow. "You don't say."

"I mean it," he said, half-laughing. "I'm allergic to asking for help. If they made a patch for it, I'd refuse to wear it."

Petra leaned forward, tapping the notebook. "Then consider this your first step in Mindset. Not proving. Just letting someone walk with you."

Her words settled in the space between them. They were simple and annoyingly true. After a pause, she added, "Your grandmother also had me keep a journal. Not for her. Not for anyone else. Just so I could hear myself more clearly. You should try it."

Tano frowned. "I don't journal."

"Then start," Petra said. "Your worth has been on lease to others' applause for too long. Writing will help you buy it back."

That night, long after the building emptied, Tano sat at his desk. He opened a fresh page, stared at it, and sighed. The scroll sat beside him, still rolled up. His grandmother's handwriting flickered in his memory, and Petra's words lingered in his ear.

Finally, he wrote:

I don't know if I can do this without proving myself. But I don't want to live like that anymore. I want to learn how to become without proving.

He set the pen down, exhaled, and closed the journal. It wasn't neat. It wasn't finished. But it was honest.

His first entry wasn't a declaration of confidence—it was a confession of dependence. Proof had been his currency for so long that imagining a life without it felt reckless. Still, he had written the words anyway.

He slipped the journal into his bag and glanced at the scroll beside it. The final line—**#67**—pressed on him, not as a sentence to reread, but as a threshold to cross.

He understood this much: deciding to stop proving wouldn't be tested in quiet moments like this one. It would be tested when it mattered.

And that test wouldn't wait.

I want to learn how to become without proving.

THE MEANING JOURNEY MODEL
MINDSET
MOMENTUM
MASTERY

Chapter 7

MINDSET IN THE MIRROR

The test came sooner than he expected. Monday morning, Tano stood in front of the mirror, his shell a little off balance and tie loose in his hand. The office was already stirring below his window, but the noise couldn't drown out the questions rising in his chest. ***If I'm not proving... what am I offering?***

He adjusted his shell, then stopped. The reflection staring back at him looked competent. Capable. Familiar. Still, the old reflex kicked in. ***Do I look like I belong? Do I look like someone they'd choose again?***

The mirror did what mirrors always do—it reflected effort, not worth. No applause. No reassurance. Just a quiet realization settling in: this was the moment his journal entry had been pointing toward. Becoming without proving didn't begin with confidence. It began with walking into the day without armor.

That afternoon, Petra found him in the rooftop garden. She set her mug down and flipped open her notebook to the triangle she had drawn. Her finger rested on the first corner. "We start here—***Mindset,***" she said. "Everything begins inside. The chase for applause, the hunger for approval—it all starts with the stories we tell ourselves. Until those shift, nothing else will." She looked up at him, eyes kind. "Rough Monday?"

Tano exhaled, glancing back toward the glass building that had reflected him that morning. "Is there any other kind?"

She smiled faintly, then tilted her head. "Tell me, Tano—what are you really looking for when you check that mirror in the morning?"

He shrugged. "I just want to look . . . right. Like I fit. Like I'm enough."

Petra set her mug down. "The problem with mirrors is simple: they don't clap. They'll show you what's there, but they'll never tell you you're worthy."

Tano frowned. "So what—ignore it? Pretend I don't care?"

Petra tilted her head. "No. I'm saying you've been chasing something mirrors can't give. Applause is a terrible landlord. It charges rent you'll never stop paying." Tano exhaled through a half-smile. "A landlord, huh?" Petra nodded. "Figures," he said quietly. "Rent's due every Monday morning."

Petra smiled, leaning in. "Exactly. You've been renting your worth from other people's approval. And rent is expensive. Alignment, on the other hand—that's ownership. Confidence doesn't come from applause. It comes from alignment. Ambition isn't the problem. Your grandmother once told me, 'Ambition with direction builds legacy. Ambition with comparison just builds exhaustion.'"

Tano's voice cracked slightly. "So it's not wrong to want more?"

"Not if it's your more," she said. "Not applause's more." The words landed—but he didn't fully embrace them.

"Easy for you to say," Tano muttered. "You're already aligned. You had her—my grandmother. You've walked this already."

Petra's smile flickered. "I'm aligned today," she said. "Ask me again next week." She leaned forward, her voice steady but still vulnerable "You think I didn't struggle? Your grandmother once asked me a question that wrecked me: 'Who are you without your title?' I sat in silence for ten minutes, terrified. Because I didn't know."

Tano looked away. He knew that feeling too well.

Petra softened. "That's the work of Mindset. It isn't neat. It's messy. You'll slip. You'll still want the applause. But the point isn't to eliminate the chase overnight. The point is to notice it. To name it. And to practice living beyond it."

Tano let her words hang in the air, then sighed. "So what you're saying is—I can't just 'Aha!' my way out of this."

Petra grinned. "Exactly. You don't flip a switch. You wrestle a story until it loosens its grip. That's Mindset."

That night, Tano stood in front of the mirror again. He whispered to himself: "Confidence doesn't come from applause. It comes from alignment." The mirror didn't answer. Didn't clap. Didn't argue. It just stared back, leaving him alone with the tension.

Later, in his journal, he wrote:

> *Today I realized my worth is still on lease. I want to believe I can buy it back, but part of me still loves the applause too much to let go. Maybe that's the point. Mindset is noticing the lease and daring to own again.*

He closed the book and exhaled. It wasn't ownership yet. But it was awareness. And awareness made him restless for action. And when the invitation arrived to lead a project no one wanted, he had to decide: chase applause or create alignment to act on what really mattered rather than what would get him noticed.

Confidence doesn't come from applause. It comes from alignment.

Chapter 8

THE PROJECT NO ONE WANTED

Awareness has a way of demanding a response. Once Tano named what he'd been renting, the question wasn't *whether* he would act—it was *where.*

That's when another email popped up on Tano's screen: "Forest International Mentoring Program—volunteer leader needed."

No one ever clicked it.

Tano stared at the blinking cursor. ***This is the kind of thing no one notices,*** he thought. ***No orb. No headlines. Just hours in a conference room with people pretending to care.*** But another whisper pressed in: ***Maybe it's the kind of thing that matters.*** He hovered over the sign-up button. Closed it. Opened it again. By the fourth time, he muttered, "I'm going to wear out my mouse before I make a decision."

When he finally told Petra that he wasn't sure if he should lead the mentoring program, she tilted her head knowingly.

"That's Mindset," she said

"It doesn't feel like Mindset," Tano replied. "It feels like volunteering for obscurity."

Petra met his gaze. "Or it could be your first step toward alignment. Applause or no applause."

He sighed. "So . . . babysitting employees in the company's most overlooked program?"

Petra smiled. "Or shaping lives in ways no one else bothers to."

Tano raised an eyebrow. "You sure this isn't just HR code for ***Congratulations, you've been volunteered***?"

Petra laughed. "Maybe. But sometimes the best projects are the ones no one fights you for."

Against his better judgment, he signed up. And, immediately, he regretted it.

The first session of mentees had five people. Four arrived on time, and one came twenty minutes late, asking if snacks were provided. The second session had six people. Two stared at their tablets the whole time. By the third, he was convinced he had made a mistake, because he wanted more people to attend so he could silently prove to others that what he was doing was worthwhile. "This is it. This is how I disappear," he muttered, head in his hands.

But then something unexpected happened.

One mentee admitted she had nearly quit Forest because no one had ever asked about her goals. Another lingered after a session just to say thank you to Tano for pairing her with a mentor who finally understood her path. He smiled faintly, remembering the scroll's words—meaning begins in small acts that outlive you. Maybe this was one of them, quietly echoing beyond what he'd see.

It wasn't fireworks. It wasn't applause. But it was something.

By week five, there were twelve people. By week seven, fourteen. Then one week, back down to six. Another week, only four. The numbers shifted unpredictably. Some weeks, the room buzzed with energy. Other weeks, it echoed with absence. Each dip gnawed at his resolve, the silence in the empty chairs louder than any applause he'd once chased.

See? No one cares. This doesn't matter, the old inner voice hissed.

Finally, one afternoon, folder in hand, he walked toward Petra's office to tell her he was done. Before he could knock, she stepped into the hallway, holding a stack of evaluations. "I was coming to find you," she said, handing him the folder.

Inside were comments scrawled in messy handwriting:

- *This is the first time I've felt seen here.*
- *I was going to leave, but now I see a future at Forest.*
- *This program gave me hope when I had none.*

Tano blinked. "These are . . . real?"

Petra nodded. "Impact isn't in the numbers. It's in the names." Her words sank deep. For the first time, the applause he craved felt strangely small. That night, he opened his journal and wrote:

Stop chasing applause. Start creating alignment.

He underlined it twice. For the first time, it felt like more than words. "Impact isn't in the numbers," Petra had told him. "It's in the names." Those words stayed with him long after the room had emptied.

He didn't know that impact would soon be tested by the one thing he couldn't control—distraction.

Stop chasing applause. Start creating alignment.

MOMENTUM

Chapter 9

MOMENTUM IN THE MARGINS

One afternoon, Harold swung by Tano's desk, grinning. "Still doing that side project? Cute. Thought you'd be aiming for the strategy task force. Real eyes on that one." Tano kept his smile measured. Harold darted off down the hallway like he always did—fast and certain the world was watching. But the words stayed with Tano long after he was gone.

That afternoon, he met with Petra. The rooftop garden had become their unspoken meeting place. Petra was already there, notebook open, tea steaming in the cool air. "Don't let loud voices shake quiet impact," she said as he sat down. "Legacy rarely shouts."

"Alright," she continued, "you've been wrestling with Mindset. You're noticing the applause, even naming it, but that's just the beginning. Now it's time for the next step." Petra turned to a fresh page in her notebook. She drew the triangle once more and, in the bottom left corner, wrote a single word: Momentum.

"This is where we go next," she said. "Momentum isn't about speed. It's about rhythm—the kind that's built through small, steady habits. The daily choices that may not look flashy but keep you moving in the right direction."

Tano raised an eyebrow. "So . . . just consistency?"

Petra smiled. "Consistency that matters. Speed gets you noticed. Rhythm gets you rooted. Everyone else is sprinting to be visible. Momentum is choosing to keep showing up in rhythm—even when no one is watching."

He folded his arms. "But what happens when it feels boring? Or too small? What if it doesn't matter?"

"That's the danger," Petra said. "Momentum rarely dies from failure. It dies from distraction. The louder, shinier opportunities that pull you away from what's meaningful. Momentum whispers, 'Keep showing up.' Distraction shouts, 'Look over here!'"

Tano smirked. "And you think I'm easily distracted?"

Petra laughed softly. "I think you're like the rest of us. Distractions call to every shell in the forest. The trick is learning which rhythm is worth protecting." She paused, looking out across the skyline. "Sometimes they still call to me," she admitted. "Especially when I'm tired. Chasing fills the calendar; creating fills the soul—and some days, the soul work feels quiet." Her voice dipped, honest and unguarded. "Even after all these years, I still catch myself glancing at what others are doing, wondering if I'm doing enough, shining enough. The old chase never fully disappears—it just lessens while changing costumes."

She smiled faintly, then said, "You know, you remind me of the old Lantern Keeper."

Tano blinked. "The what?"

"The Lantern Keeper," she repeated, leaning back. "It's a story my grandmother told me when I was younger—and again not long after I started here at Forest International, when I was chasing every project I thought would make me stand out."

She cleared her throat, her voice softening. "There was once a Lantern Keeper who tended the great lamp at the edge of the forest. Her task was simple: light it at dusk, keep it burning through the night, and let it rest at dawn so travelers could find their way home. After a few months, she began to crave something more—something memorable. So she mixed new oils, built higher flames, tried to make her lamp the brightest anyone had ever seen. And for a while, it worked. The whole valley talked about that brilliant light."

"But the brighter she burned it," she continued, "the faster it dimmed. One night, the lamp failed completely, and travelers wandered lost in the dark. The Keeper sat there in silence, ashamed and exhausted. Her apprentice—a young owl sat beside her and said, 'They don't remember how bright it burned. They remember that it was always there.'"

Tano looked down, tracing the rim of his mug. "That's… familiar." His voice was low, almost surprised at how much the words hit home.

Petra gave a knowing smile, then continued. "After that, the Keeper stopped chasing the shine and started tending the light. Each evening, she showed up, lit the lamp, and tended it with quiet care. The light wasn't the brightest anymore, but it never failed again. Years later, travelers would say, 'There was always a light waiting for us when the road was long.' They didn't know her name—but they trusted her rhythm."

Petra let the story settle between them. Her eyes reflected the city's faint glow.

"I used to be that Keeper," she said quietly. "Always turning the flame higher. Always thinking if I just worked harder, someone would finally notice. But I learned the hard way that the brighter you burn, the faster you break—and burnout never brings applause." She gave a small, self-aware laugh. "I still forget sometimes."

She looked down at her mug, the steam curling between them. "For the longest time, I thought living a meaningful life meant going somewhere far away," she admitted. "A years-long journey, a silent retreat in the woods, something epic enough to prove I'd finally found myself." She smiled softly. "But meaning isn't hiding out there—it's built in here," she said, tapping her chest. "It's created in the small, intentional steps we choose each day. The quiet ones no one claps for, but that slowly shape who we're becoming." She exhaled. "That's what the Lantern Keeper learned. That's what I'm still learning."

Tano watched the steam rise from her mug and wondered how many nights she'd spent tending her own unseen light. Tano looked down at his shell, tracing one of the faint grooves near its edge. "So maybe the goal isn't to outshine everyone else."

Petra smiled. "No. The goal is to keep the light alive."

Silence filled the space again—comfortable this time. The floor was empty now, the last voices long gone. Outside, the late-night lights of Forest International glowed steadily across the campus, each window a quiet promise against the dark. Tano took a slow breath. "I think I've been trying to be the flame everyone notices," he said. "Maybe it's time I learn to be the one that never goes out."

Petra nodded, her eyes warm. "That's momentum, Tano. That's the start of creating rhythm." Petra's voice softened. "Remember, Tano—busyness is noise. Rhythm is music. You'll have to choose which one you're making." Her words followed him down the stairs that day, echoing louder than the footsteps of those rushing to their next meeting.

Tano didn't know it yet, but the test of distraction was closer than he thought.

Chapter 10

THE QUIET WORK OF MOMENTUM

The first real test of rhythm didn't come from the work. It came from someone Tano trusted.

The next week, with her characteristic grin, Lina found Tano in the breakroom, leaning against the counter. "Heard you're still running that old mentoring thing," Lina said. "Yeah," Tano replied, cautious.

Lina sipped her tea and tilted her head. "Can I be honest? Why waste your time? Leadership doesn't care about it. It's not going anywhere. But there's a task force starting next month—cross-department, high visibility, all the right people watching. That's how you get noticed. That's how you move up. You should apply for the task force instead."

The words landed like a weight. Not cruel. Not dismissive. Just tempting. Lina wasn't wrong—visibility was currency at Forest International. And part of Tano still craved it.

That afternoon, he sat at his desk staring at the mentoring calendar. He thought, ***Maybe Lina's right. Maybe I should switch. Maybe it's time to stop hiding in the***

margins and step into something people actually notice.

The next session made the decision to continue leading the Mentoring program much harder. Four people showed up. Four. He looked at the empty chairs and thought, ***This is pointless. All this work, and for what?***

The week after, there were six. Then fourteen. Then back to seven. The numbers rose and fell like the tide, tugging his confidence with them. Each dip was a whisper: ***See? No one cares. This doesn't matter.***

One afternoon he opened Petra's office door, frustration written all over his face. "I don't get it. Some weeks attendance at my mentoring meetings grows, the next it shrinks. It feels like I'm running in place."

Petra set her mug down. "And yet, you keep showing up."

"Yeah, but maybe I should take Lina's advice. That task force—"

Petra cut him off with a gentle shake of her head. "Momentum isn't built by fireworks, Tano. It's not about crowds or claps. ***Momentum is choosing the rhythm even when the numbers wobble. Distraction will always promise more visibility. But rhythm will always give more meaning.***"

Tano exhaled, half-smiling. "So what you're saying is . . . no fireworks? Great. I finally learn consistency, and it doesn't even come with sparklers."

Petra laughed softly. "You'll thank me, when you stop catching fire."

Her words lingered longer than the doubts. So he kept going. Week after week. Sometimes fourteen. Sometimes four. No orb camera following them around for everyone to see. No applause. Just steady lunchtime mentoring meetings where stories were told, where people felt seen, where belonging grew quietly.

One mentee lingered afterward and said, "Thanks, Tano. This is the only space I feel like I belong here." Those words steadied him more than a standing ovation ever could.

That night, Tano opened his journal and wrote:

> *Stop chasing busyness. Start creating rhythm.*

He underlined "rhythm" until the ink pressed through the page. For the first time, the word didn't feel like something he was striving for. It felt like something he was already living.

But momentum without recognition would soon meet its toughest opponent—silence.

Chapter 11

MASTERY IN THE SILENCE

The mentoring lunches had settled into their own quiet rhythm. Some weeks the table was full, other weeks it felt sparse. But each time, stories spilled across sandwiches, and laughter softened the cafeteria corners.

Still, the old voice whispered to Tano: ***Does this really matter? What if Lina's right? What if I'm wasting my time?***

One afternoon, Petra waved him up to join her on the rooftop garden. Her notebook was already open, triangle in the margin. She tapped the final corner with her finger and wrote the word clearly: **Mastery.**

"This is the last stage," she said. "Mastery isn't about being the best. It's about persistence. It's about the habits of resilience—the daily choice to keep showing up when everything around you tells you it's pointless. When the crowd is gone. When even the people closest to you don't understand."

Tano frowned. "Persisting without applause?"

"Exactly," Petra said. "**Resilience is rhythm under pressure.** Not just when you're tired. But when you're doubted."

Her voice softened. "Let me tell you a story."

She stared into her tea as if rewinding years with her eyes. "I once led a community project outside of Forest International. It meant the world to me. I gave evenings, weekends, energy I didn't have. And then one night, my mom called. She asked why I was wasting my time on something so small, something that wouldn't advance my career. She told me she wanted me to make the family proud. She couldn't see the value in what I was building."

Her voice faltered for a moment before continuing. "I tried to explain, but halfway through, I realized I wasn't angry with her—I was still chasing her applause. Even after all these years."

She looked out across the garden, her eyes glistening. "Your grandmother once told me that chasing love is the loneliest kind of exhaustion. She said, ***'Create from who you are, not from who someone else needs you to be.'*** That line has followed me ever since. It didn't fix the ache, but it gave me rhythm again." Her voice softened. "I used to think healing meant reconciliation. Now I know sometimes it just means peace with the unanswered parts."

She drew in a slow breath. "I almost quit that night. Because nothing cuts deeper than realizing someone you love doesn't understand the rhythm you're called to create."

Tano sat in silence, his chest heavy. He thought of his own father's absence. Of every time he had longed for a voice saying, ***"I see you. I'm proud of you."*** He couldn't imagine hearing the opposite—from someone who was actually present.

Petra continued. "Your grandmother told me something I'll never forget. She said: ***'Sometimes the people who love us the most understand us the least.'*** That was when I learned Mastery. Not because I got it right. But because I didn't quit." She closed her notebook. "That's the work ahead of you. Not applause. Not visibility. Mastery. **Roots that hold when storms rage.**"

Tano gave a small, crooked smile. "So . . . less fireworks, more photosynthesis?"

Petra chuckled. "Exactly. Growth that happens underground."

Tano leaned forward, voice low. "So if Mindset was buying back my worth, and Momentum was choosing rhythm, then Mastery is . . . what? Just surviving the hard?"

Petra shook her head. "No. Mastery isn't surviving the hard. It's being shaped by it. **It's letting the struggle forge the strength you couldn't get any other way.**" The words sank deep, but Tano couldn't shake the ache in his chest. He wanted to believe he could live them.

That night, he opened his journal but didn't write anything. He stared at the page, the pen hovering.

Mastery without applause.

He whispered the phrase aloud. The silence didn't answer.

But for the first time, he wondered: *Could silence itself be an answer?* He was about to find out—because silence was coming for everything he'd built.

PROGRAM
CANCELLED

Chapter 12

ROOTED IN MASTERY

The email message arrived at 6:12 a.m. on Tano's phone, before the sun warmed the glass of Forest International:

> *Subject: Program Consolidation & Budget Alignment*

Tano opened it on instinct. He didn't make it past the second paragraph.

> ***Effective immediately, the Forest International Mentoring Program will be discontinued. We appreciate the volunteers who contributed to its run and encourage teams to focus on core priorities aligned to near-term outcomes.***

He read it again. Then a third time, slower, as if the words might soften if they felt seen.

Discontinued. Not paused. Not reimagined. Cut.

He stared at the screen, a pulse in his temple keeping time with the ache in his chest. He pictured the circle of chairs. The awkward first ten minutes that always, somehow, turned honest. He pictured the note in uneven handwriting: ***This is the first time I've felt seen at Forest.***

A door opened behind him. "Morning," Lina said lightly, sliding to the edge of his desk. "You see the note?" She didn't wait. "Listen—don't get pulled under with this. I told you leadership didn't care. And I have good news: the task force is official. Cross-department. Big audience. I can get your name on the list today." She smiled like she was handing him a life raft.

He looked up slowly. "They cut it," he said, as if she couldn't read.

"I know," Lina said, softer. "I also know you. You care. But you don't have to drown here. Take the step that moves you forward. Be seen. Come with me."

The offer should have felt like oxygen. Instead, it tasted like dust. "I'll think about it," he said. He meant it... and he didn't.

After she left, he walked the long way to Petra's office, past framed campaign posters and glossy photos from launches that trended for a week and vanished the next. He knocked. Petra waved him in, already holding a mug he suspected had been poured for him.

"I saw," she said.

"It's gone," he answered.

She nodded. "This is where Mastery begins."

He laughed once, too sharp to be humor. "It feels like where it ends."

Petra set the mug down. "Do you remember what I told you about my mother?"

He did. ***Why are you wasting your time on something that won't advance your career? Don't you want to make the family proud?***

"Painful questions rarely come from enemies," Petra said. "They come from people who love us, but don't see what we're building."

Tano swallowed. "What if no one sees? What if it really doesn't matter?"

Petra's gaze didn't wobble. "Then you have to decide who you're becoming in the dark." He breathed out slowly. Confidence doesn't come from applause; it comes from alignment. The scroll had said it, Petra had echoed it, and now he finally felt it.

He looked away, out toward the hallway, where the day kept walking as if nothing had happened. The hallway blurred, the sound of footsteps fading into memory. He thought of another doorway long ago—a smaller one, framed by the outline of a father who never quite fit inside it. That was the first silence he'd ever known, the kind that taught him to earn attention instead of receive it.

For years, that absence had chased him through every project, every polished slide, every invisible achievement. But standing here now, he realized something he never could as a child: the absence wasn't his fault, and it no longer had to define his worth.

Maybe some echoes only stop when you choose to stop running from them. The words hung in the air like truth long overdue—one he had spent a lifetime outrunning.

In the window's reflection, he saw his own shell, smaller than it felt. The memory cracked open—the silence that followed his questions, the invisible measuring stick he had been chasing since he was old enough to crave the words, ***I see you. I'm proud of you.*** For years, the chase had been about filling that space. Today, the space still existed, but it no longer owned him.

"Lina offered me a seat on a task force," he said quietly. "High visibility. Senior eyes."

"And does it align?" Petra asked.

He hated how fast the answer arrived. "No."

She nodded once. "Then it's just noise, in a moment that asks for music."

He closed his eyes. Mastery wasn't dramatic. It wasn't triumphant. It was the ache of standing still when every impulse begged him to sprint back to applause.

Tano rubbed the small drum in his palm. "What do I do?"

"What you already know," Petra said. "Not the program. The people. The rhythm underneath the program that never needed a budget to exist."

Petra reached into her drawer and pulled out a small keychain drum—hand-carved, worn smooth from time. "Your grandmother gave me this when I hit my own Mastery wall," she said, pressing it into his palm. "To remind me: rhythm doesn't end when the music fades. It deepens."

Tano turned it over. "Finally—a percussion instrument for meetings that could use rhythm."

Petra grinned. "Just don't start a drum circle in Finance."

Tano turned his attention to the mini drum, turning it over gently. The wood felt warm. Real. Steady.

That evening, Ama handed him tea without a word. But this time, she didn't ask why he was late or what he had said no to. She just sat beside him—no tension, no disappointment. Just presence.

And this time, he didn't miss how she showed up for him.

All those years of chasing applause from people who barely knew his name—and here was the one who had waited. The one he had drifted from while trying to feel seen. He wondered how many moments like this he'd traded away—and how many he still had time to choose.

And in that quiet, he realized something had shifted. Not everything. But enough.

The next morning, he sent a message anyway, hands trembling: ***"Lunch. My treat. Thursday. Same time."***

Five showed up. They looked unsure, until the first story cracked a smile out of the room. The next week, seven. Then four. Then eleven. The numbers wobbled, but the rhythm didn't.

Lina caught him by the elevators a few days later. "You're really going to keep this up?" she asked, not unkindly, just incredulous. "Off the clock? Off the books?"

He met her eyes. "It matters."

She shifted her weight. "I don't get it."

He nodded. "I know." She didn't push. Good friends sometimes don't. They just leave a door open and a light on.

At the end of the month, one of the mentees—Imani, the quiet analyst who rarely spoke above a hum—handed him a note folded into a small square. He opened it at his desk.

> *I stayed because someone asked me why I was here and meant it. Thank you.*

He read it twice. For the first time in weeks, the work felt undeniably real and meaningful.

That evening, as office lights clicked off in pockets and the city softened to its evening color, Tano opened his journal. He stared at the blank page for a long breath, then wrote slowly, pressing each word into the paper as if he were carving it into wood:

> *Stop chasing comfort. Start creating resilience.*

He paused, then added beneath it:

> *Comfort looks like applause and easy exits.*
> *Resilience looks like showing up when the budget doesn't.*
> *I'm tired of proving. I'm ready to persist.*

He closed the journal. The ache was still there. So was the uncertainty. But underneath both, something steadier had taken root. Not loud. Not quick. Just a rhythm that held. And somewhere beyond that rhythm, a familiar sound stirred again: a starting whistle.

Stop chasing comfort. Start creating resilience.

START

Chapter 13

THE STARTING LINE AGAIN

Over time, the mentoring meetings stopped being something he hosted and became something people leaned into. This one started with a question.

David, one of the newer mentees, lingered after a mentoring lunch. He fidgeted with his pen before blurting out, "That race you quit . . . the Trailblazer one. Did it feel like failing?"

Tano smiled—not out of performance, but out of peace. "It felt like losing," he admitted. "Until I realized I was only losing something I never needed to chase in the first place."

David hesitated. "Would you ever run it again?"

Tano paused—not for effect, but for truth. "Maybe. But only if I could run it differently. Not for applause. For alignment."

A few days later, Petra pulled him aside. "Did you hear? Three other departments started their own mentoring lunches. Said it began after hearing your story." Tano smiled, warmth spreading quietly through his chest. He didn't say anything, but he applauded for himself on the inside—something he'd learned from her.

Two weeks later, the announcement went live across Forest International's feed:

> **Trailblazer Race Returns—One Day. One Course. One Opportunity to Lead.**

At first, the post barely caused a ripple. Most assumed it was a rebrand of the old competition—a leadership PR moment more than a true test. But then the rumor spread: **Harold had signed up.**

That changed everything.

By the end of the first day, not a single other name had appeared on the roster. Forest buzzed with rumors, most saying what everyone already believed—Harold would win before the rest even started. Alone at his desk, Tano opened the Trailblazer page. He hovered over the sign-up button, fingers resting on the keys. He glanced at the scroll in his drawer. "#67," he whispered. "Maybe this is mine."

He clicked the sign-up button.

Late in the workday, as the office lights dimmed and the feed refreshed, another name appeared—quietly, almost defiantly.

> **Tano.**

Some thought it was a mistake. Others assumed he'd withdraw by morning. But he didn't.

And just like that, the story began to shift.

Whispers spread through hallways and chat threads.
"Isn't that the guy who quit the first race?"

"He's running again?"
"Why would he do that?"

They didn't understand. He wasn't running to win anymore. He was running to finish. This wasn't about Harold. It was about courage—the kind that doesn't trend or boast, the kind that quietly shows up to finish what it once walked away from. He was choosing alignment—letting what he believed guide what he did, even when no one was watching—and that choice alone felt like victory. The forest clearing looked the same as before—banners strung high, the orb camera hovering like an unblinking eye. But this time, there were no crowds pressing in. No spectacle. No noise.

Just two names on the roster.

Tano.

Harold.

The tortoise and the hare. Just like the old story. But completely different.

For days, Forest buzzed. Some called it brave, others foolish. A few whispered that Tano was walking straight into another humiliation. But Tano didn't read the intra company threads. He simply walked the trails before dawn, synchronizing his breath to the rhythm of his small hand drum—not training for speed, but practicing peace.

When race day came, the forest clearing stirred again—banners high, orb camera humming, crowd hushed with curiosity.

Two competitors. Two stories. The same starting line.

Harold stretched, bouncing on his toes with energy to spare. "You ready to lose again, old friend?" he called, his grin already chasing the orb camera.

Tano smiled—not big, but steady. "This time, I'm not racing you."

Harold laughed. "That's what they all say before they lose."

The orb camera tilted closer. The countdown loomed. Tano reached into his shell and touched the bark card Petra had given him—her quiet wisdom now etched into his bones:

> **Not all applause is alignment. Not all alignment needs applause.**

The small hand-carved drum Petra gifted him hung from his strap, a rhythm reminder of significant meaning. He smiled, thinking of Petra—the HR badger who had learned to stop chasing her mother's applause so that others could learn to stop chasing theirs. He hoped she knew how many lives she'd lightened—one conversation, one honest story at a time.

He carried more than a card and a drum. He carried the work itself:

- The **Mindset** of owning his worth instead of renting it from applause
- The **Momentum** of steady mentoring and meaningful rhythm
- The **Mastery** of showing up when no one was watching

The ache of his father's absence was still there. The silence hadn't vanished. Lina's doubts still whispered to him from time to time. But none of them were steering his path anymore. They were passengers on his journey.

For the first time, Tano no longer needed the race to answer the question of who he was. He closed his eyes and breathed in the forest air—steady, grounded, free. And in that quiet, he could almost hear his grandmother again—her voice, soft but certain, carrying the words she once whispered as a hope for him:

> *I will stop chasing what fades.*
> *I will start creating what lasts.*
> *I will walk steady in alignment, rhythm, and resilience.*
> *This is my race. This is my pace.*

He smiled—not because others were watching, but because he finally believed her.

The forest fell silent. Even the orb camera seemed to hold its breath.

The announcer's voice cut through the hush, clear and commanding: "On your mark . . ."

Tano's heart steadied. Breathe in. Breathe out.

"Get ready . . ."

He closed his eyes for a beat, the word create forming silently on his tongue—the one that had carried him this far.

"Set . . ."

A single exhale. A whisper only he could hear.

"Create."

The whistle split the silence. And with it, the race—and a new kind of beginning—began.

Harold shot forward like a headline. The orb camera followed close behind.

Tano crouched. Not to launch. To root. Then he moved. Steady. Aligned. Creating every step. This wasn't the desperate rhythm of someone chasing. It was the quiet confidence of someone creating.

Partway down the trail, Harold glanced back, smirking as if to say, ***"You'll never catch me."*** Tano smiled, but not at Harold. At himself. Because he wasn't running to catch anyone anymore. He wasn't running to win. He was running to grow.

The orb camera followed Harold as he pulled farther ahead, soaking in the spotlight like sunlight. Confident. Certain. Until certainty turned careless. By mile four, the Hare slowed, stretched, and yawned. "I've got this in the bag," he muttered, lowering himself against a shaded tree. The orb camera hovered uncertainly, recording as he closed his eyes. "Just a quick nap," he said aloud, as if victory could wait.

Tano passed quietly minutes later. He didn't gloat. Didn't glance. Just kept his rhythm—step, breath, step—his grandmother's words echoing deep inside: ***Steady is enough.***

Then, behind him, a sound split the stillness. Leaves rustled. Branches snapped. Harold's voice cut through the woods. "Wait—what?!" The Hare bolted upright, eyes wide. The orb camera swung back just in time to catch him scramble to his feet. Panic surged through him as realization hit—Tano was almost at the final bend.

Harold ran like thunder, legs blurring, dust rising in furious clouds. His breath came ragged, eyes fixed ahead—on the small, steady shell moving closer and closer to the finish.

The crowd gasped. The orb camera split its focus—one lens on Harold's sprint, the other on Tano's unwavering rhythm. Every viewer leaned forward, caught between flash and faith. The forest seemed to lean in too, branches bowing toward the trail as the two figures closed the distance.

Harold was closing the gap. The distance shrank from yards to feet. The roar of his steps echoed like a drumbeat of desperation. But Tano didn't turn. Didn't flinch. Didn't break rhythm.

Step. Breath. Step. Breath.

He crossed the final clearing as the sun hit the horizon—light spilling over him like gold.

One more step. Then another. Then the finish line beneath his shell. The orb camera froze on the image—Tano still moving, even after the race was done.

Harold stumbled into the clearing seconds later, skidding to a stop, panting, eyes wide with disbelief.

The crowd erupted. ***The Tortoise beat the Hare.***

But Tano didn't raise his arms. Didn't gloat. He simply exhaled—a long, quiet breath that had been waiting years to leave him. As Tano caught his breath, Harold approached, chest heaving.

"Didn't see that coming," Harold said, grinning. "But maybe . . . you were running the right race all along."

Tano smiled. "I was."

Tano didn't notice the tears at first. They came quietly, tracing lines along the curve of his shell. They weren't born of sadness, but of release—the kind that comes when years of proving finally meet peace. Each drop felt like a letting go: of applause, of comparison, of the need to be seen. The earth beneath him drank them in, as if it understood. And when he finally looked up, the world seemed clearer—not because it had changed, but because he had.

While the world celebrated a victory, Tano celebrated something else: that he had finished what he once quit. The cheers faded, but the quiet stayed. In that stillness, a memory rose—the outline of a doorway, the shadow of a father who had promised to return but never did. For years, that absence had set his pace. Every project, every late night, every polished slide had been an unspoken sprint to earn the words he'd never heard: ***I see you. I'm proud of you.***

He felt the hurt, but it no longer ruled him. This race had never really been about Harold—it had always been about himself, the boy still running for a father who never turned back. Every step today had been an act of release, not anger. A reclaiming. For years, he had run to prove he was worth staying for. Today, he ran because he finally believed he was.

That belief changed everything. The emptiness that once pushed him forward now pulled him home. It became the reason he showed up for his children—reading one more story, lingering one more minute, listening one more time. He wasn't outrunning his father's shadow anymore. Instead, he was becoming the light that would guide his own kids. He had learned that healing isn't about erasing what hurt you; it's about refusing to let it define you.

So, with every bedtime story and every ordinary moment, he was quietly rewriting what love looked like. He was building a legacy where presence mattered more than perfection. And now, with every small act of showing up, he was creating something his father never could—a rhythm of belonging that would outlast him. Every step carried the weight of rhythm, of legacy, of the impact of #67 he still carried close to his shell.

He knew one day he would tell his children—not about winning or losing, but about choosing to stay, to listen, and to build something that didn't need applause to matter. He knew one day he would tell his children. Not today. Maybe tomorrow.

The race was over. But the creating—that was just beginning.

TOMORROW

TOMORROW'S STORY

Moonlight slipped through the window as Tano sat beside the bed, one hand resting gently on the shell of the smallest. Four shells were tucked beneath blankets, eyes heavy but resisting sleep just a little longer.

The story had ended. His presence had not. A voice rose from the pillows—soft, sincere, and honestly puzzled.

"Dadda, I love your story . . . but I have no idea what *'synergy'* even means."

Tano laughed—the kind of laugh that only comes after something sacred has settled.

"To be honest," he whispered, "neither did I—or anyone at Forest."

The other three stirred, half-awake, and Tano lowered his voice.

"Alright," he said softly, "you know what comes next."

Groans filled the room.

"Do we *have* to, Dadda?" one of the twins moaned.

"Yes," Tano said with a grin. "Especially when you don't feel like it. Ready?"

Together, in a jumble of tired voices, they recited the words that had become their nightly rhythm:

> *I will stop chasing what fades.*
> *I will start creating what lasts.*
> *I will walk steady in alignment, rhythm, and resilience.*
> *This is my race. This is my pace.*

The twins collapsed into giggles at the last line, the oldest rolled his eyes, and his baby girl whispered, "I like 'walk steady'—but I want to run!"

Tano smiled. "You can," he said. "Just make sure you're running toward something real."

He kissed their foreheads one by one. He had started the ritual for them, but somewhere along the way, it had started shaping him, too. When he stepped into the hallway, Ama was waiting—tea in hand, a tired but contented smile on her face. No words, just the kind of silence that used to feel like distance but now felt like peace. Tano reached for Ama's hand, and they stood there for a moment, listening to the laughter that still echoed from the kids' room—a rhythm he hadn't heard in years.

Then, from inside, his baby girl's voice cut through the quiet again. "But Dadda . . . what about the last one? What was #67?"

Tano glanced at Ama, who smiled knowingly. He squeezed Ama's hand once and stepped back into the room. The room went still. Tano smiled softly, the same way his grandmother once had. "#67?" he repeated. "That one's special."

His baby girl leaned closer. "What is it?"

He tucked the blanket under her chin and whispered, "When I found the scroll, #67 was blank. At first, I thought something was missing—but then I realized it wasn't empty. It was waiting."

Her eyes widened. "Waiting for what?"

Tano smiled. "For me. For you. For all of us." He continued softly, "Each of us gets our own #67. It's the wisdom we create from how we live—the moment we stop chasing and start creating. Sometimes it marks a shift we've already made; sometimes it's the one we're still reaching for. But either way, it's ours to write." He paused, brushing a strand of hair from her forehead. "Your #67 becomes a marker of meaning—a reminder that the story isn't over, it's unfolding."

His princess smiled sleepily. "Tomorrow, then?"

He nodded. "Yes, tomorrow."

As the light clicked off, the room settled into the soft rhythm of their breathing. The night didn't feel like an ending anymore—it felt like a beginning. And maybe that was the point—that #67 was never meant to finish a story, but to start one.

Not just for Tano. For all of us.

He leaned back in the dark, listening to the steady beat of their breathing. There was still one part of the old story he hadn't told them—the deeper reason he kept going in the Big Race with the Hare. But that, he decided, would have to wait for another bedtime story…

Tano's story may have ended here—but yours is just beginning. The journey from chasing to creating isn't finished with one race. It's lived every day—in small, steady choices. That's why the next section begins with a pledge: a declaration to stop chasing what fades and start creating what lasts. After that, you'll have the space to reflect, take action, and even write your own #67.

THE PRACTICE

THE RACE CONTINUES WITH YOU

"MY RACE, MY PACE" PLEDGE

The journey doesn't end with Tano. It continues with you.

This pledge is an invitation—a chance to step fully out of chasing and into creating.

- The **Full Pledge** is something you declare once and sign—a marker of commitment you can return to whenever the old chase calls your name.
- The **Daily Recitation** is something you can carry with you—a rhythm to repeat each morning, before a meeting, or whenever you need to return to alignment.

Both are yours. Speak them. Live them. Let them steady your steps.

The Full Pledge

I choose to stop chasing what fades
and start creating what lasts.

I refuse to measure my worth by applause, titles, or speed.
My worth is rooted in alignment, rhythm, and resilience.

I will walk my journey with steady, courageous steps—
not for recognition,
but for a legacy of meaning.

I will not run another's race.
I will not bow to another's pace.
I will live **my race, my pace**—
with purpose, with presence, with peace.

Signed: ____________________

Date: ____________________

The Daily Pledge

For every morning, every reset, every moment you need to remember (like Tano and his kids):

> *I will stop chasing what fades.*
> *I will start creating what lasts.*
> *I will walk steady in alignment, rhythm, and resilience.*
> ***This is my race. This is my pace.***

YOUR #67

The scroll ended with #67. But it wasn't finished. At first, Tano wondered if it was a mistake—a line left blank. But the more he looked, the more he realized: the emptiness was the point.

Because #67 isn't handed down. It's created. It isn't someone else's wisdom to follow. It's yours to shape.

This space is your invitation to create the wisdom you need most right now—a shift from **chasing** to **creating.**

Two ways to write your #67:

- **Stop/Start Statement**
  A clear shift from what you've been chasing to what you want to create.
  - *Example from my own journey:*
    For years, I played it safe, chasing acceptance so that I wouldn't be rejected. But safety shrank me. Creating means stepping out, even when rejection is possible, because meaning is worth the risk.
    #67—Stop chasing safety. Start creating courage.
- **Poetic Proverb**
  A timeless saying important enough that it would be shared for many generations.
  - *Example:*
    The shell grows strongest when it dares to crack open.

Now it's your turn.

What wisdom does your "shell" need to carry?
What will your #67 be?

For more stories, prompts, and ways to share your #67 with others, visit **ThisIsMy67.com**.

HOW TO USE THIS BOOK FOR BOOK CLUBS, TEAMS, OR PERSONAL GROWTH

Before you dive into the reflection questions, here's a simple guide to help you make *Stop Chasing, Start Creating* work in your life—whether you're reading it on your own, with a small group, or inside your organization. There's no single "right" way to walk this journey—only what works best for your rhythm, your people, and your purpose. The rhythm matters more than the rules.

1. **The Four- to Six-Week Journey**

Read two to three chapters per week. Use the reflection questions to spark honest conversation about how the story connects to your own work and life. End each session by identifying one small, aligned action to try before the next meeting.

2. The Meaningful Lunch Series

Host a weekly or biweekly "Meaningful Lunch." Read one chapter or section aloud (or listen to the audiobook), then discuss one or two questions that stand out. Keep it relaxed—no slides, just stories and takeaways.

3. The Team Retreat Experience

For leadership retreats or team development days, focus on ***The Letter and the Legacy*** and the chapters where the ***Meaning Journey Model*** is mentioned. Use them as anchors for deeper reflection on your organization's culture, rhythm, and resilience.

4. The Continuous Rhythm

After finishing the book, revisit one principle or reflection question each month as an ongoing team rhythm. Growth isn't a one-time sprint; it's a steady walk of alignment, rhythm, and resilience.

However you choose to use this book, make it yours.
Adapt the pace, choose the questions that resonate most, and keep the focus simple:
Stop chasing what fades. Start creating what lasts—together.

FOR CORPORATE AND LEADERSHIP BOOK CLUBS

If you're leading this book within your company, team, or leadership cohort, consider a few facilitation practices that make the most of the journey:

- **Create safety first.** Start each session with a positive focus or short story of meaning.
- **Model vulnerability.** Share your own "chasing versus creating" moment to invite authenticity.
- **Honor every voice.** Let silence be part of the learning—meaning grows in the pause.
- **End with action.** Always close by identifying one small, aligned next step for each participant or for the team.

SUGGESTED FORMAT (45–60 MINUTES)

1. **Opening (10 minutes)**—What's been positive in your life + short excerpt
2. **Discussion (25–35 minutes)**—Three to four reflection questions tied to workplace meaning or leadership culture
3. **Application (5–10 minutes)**—One small step or commitment per person
4. **Closing (5 minutes)**—End with the *Daily Recitation:*

   I will stop chasing what fades.
   I will start creating what lasts.
   I will walk steady in alignment, rhythm, and resilience.
   This is my race. This is my pace.

WANT TO GO DEEPER?

For a more in-depth **Facilitator and Leader Guide**—including sample pacing, weekly outlines, and printable discussion templates—contact us at **Meaningful365.com.**

Together, let's help more teams stop chasing what fades and start creating what lasts.

REFLECTION QUESTIONS

Stories move us, but reflection shapes us. Tano's story invites you to slow down and notice your own.

These questions are here as invitations—for journaling, for honest conversations, or for team discussions. Each one is designed not just to help you reflect but to help you practice the shift from chasing to creating. Meaning grows deeper when you pause long enough to ask the right questions.

THE STORY BEFORE THE STORY

- What story do people often tell about you—and how is it different from the story you wish they knew?
- When have you accepted a label (like "slow") that came from comparison instead of truth?
- If you had to name your "steady"—the quality you choose to embrace no matter what others call it—what would it be?

CHAPTER 1

- In what areas of your life are you tempted to polish your "shell" so that people like you but don't really see you?
- What is on your own "Almost Said" list that you've been resisting saying out loud?
- What would alignment—not applause—look like in your everyday life (professionally or personally)?

CHAPTER 2

- When have you engineered an impression rather than speaking your truth?
- How much energy do you spend on being visible versus being authentic?
- What might shift if you focused less on presentation and more on presence?

CHAPTER 3

- What "race" are you currently running, and whose expectations set the pace?
- Have you ever shown up using someone else's definition of success instead of your own? What did that require you to silence, adjust, or hide about yourself?
- How do you define "enough," and who gave you that definition?

CHAPTER 4

* When have you stepped away from something because your identity was tied to winning?
* What voices of comparison keep disrupting your rhythm?
* How do you respond when silence feels louder than applause?

CHAPTER 5

* What wisdom or legacy has been passed down to you, and how has it shaped you?
* Which saying (or truth) from your own life has steadied you when applause failed?
* How might the mystery of #67 invite you to live differently, even before you can name it?

CHAPTER 6

* In what areas are you still proving instead of becoming?
* What would it look like to ask for help, even when it feels uncomfortable?
* How could journaling—honestly, not perfectly—help you hear your own voice?

CHAPTER 7

- ✸ What "mirror moments" reveal how much you depend on applause?
- ✸ In what areas are you renting your worth from other people's approval?
- ✸ What step could help you buy back your sense of worth through alignment?

CHAPTER 8

- ✸ What small, unnoticed project might be your version of the mentoring program?
- ✸ How do you discern when to choose alignment even when it isn't visible?
- ✸ What would it mean for you to stop chasing applause and start creating alignment?

CHAPTER 9

- ✸ Where do distractions tempt you away from what matters most?
- ✸ How do you confuse busyness with meaning?
- ✸ What rhythms could you create to keep showing up, even when it isn't exciting?

CHAPTER 10

- ✸ How do fluctuating "numbers" (likes, attendance, recognition) affect your confidence?

- In what areas of your life do you need to trust rhythm more than results?
- What would it look like to stop chasing busyness and start creating rhythm?

CHAPTER 11

- When have people closest to you misunderstood or questioned your meaningful work?
- How do you handle doubt—both yours and others'?
- What might it mean to let struggle *shape* you, not just wear you down?

CHAPTER 12

- In what circumstances have you been tempted to quit because of a disruption outside your control?
- What voices—past or present—make resilience harder for you to achieve?
- What would it look like to stop chasing comfort and start creating resilience?

CHAPTER 13

- In what area are you being invited to return to something you once quit—but differently this time?
- What is your "secret reason" to finish, which no one else can see but you?

- How can you run with rhythm instead of rushing toward recognition?

TOMORROW'S STORY

- What did the bedtime ending stir in you—about legacy, laughter, and mystery?
- What is your #67—the wisdom shift from chasing to creating—that only you can write?
- If tomorrow is inviting you to stop chasing and start creating, what one small step can you take *today* to begin living that shift?

THE CREATING CHECKPOINTS

Tano's journey wasn't only about races or meetings at Forest International. It was about the small, steady choices he made each day—the kind of choices we all face.

The following Creating Checkpoints rise from his story and are offered for yours. They are invitations: questions to pause on, wisdom to wrestle with, and actions to practice in your own rhythm.

Meaning isn't found in one big moment. It's created in the steps you choose again and again.

1. **Mindset (Internal Compass)**

Shifting from chasing external signals → to creating inner strength

Value over Virality

> Would I post this if no one commented—but it genuinely encouraged or helped someone who read it silently?

→ Impressions fade quickly. Impact remains—even when no one is watching.

Action: Share something this week with no expectation of likes or comments—simply because it's true and could help one person.

Impact over Titles

Would I still pursue this role if it came without a title—but gave me the chance to make real change?

→ Titles decorate résumés, but impact shapes legacies.

Action: Write down one way you can make a difference today that has nothing to do with your position or role. Do it quietly.

Curiosity over Certainty

Would I still listen if I couldn't win the argument—but I might learn something new?

→ Certainty ends the conversation; curiosity invites transformation.

Action: In your next disagreement, ask one question instead of making one point.

Integrity over Image

Would I still act this way if nobody noticed—but I knew I stayed true to myself?

→ Images can be polished, but integrity makes you whole.

Action: Choose one decision this week that no one will see but you—and honor it anyway.

Patience over Speed

Would I still commit if it took years to bear fruit—but the outcome was truly meaningful?

→ Speed excites, but patience produces lasting meaning.

Action: Identify one long-term goal you've been rushing. Take one small step toward it today, without forcing quick results.

2. Momentum (Daily Rhythm and Habits)

Moving from distraction and hustle → to intentional rhythm and growth.

Progress over Perfection

Would I still start this if I knew I might stumble—but each step moved me forward?

→ Perfection stalls momentum; imperfect steps create movement that compounds.

Action: Start something you've been delaying until it was "perfect." Take one imperfect step today.

Alignment over Activity

Would I still add this to my schedule if it didn't make me look busy—but it aligned with what matters most?

→ Activity fills calendars, but alignment fuels purpose.

Action: Review tomorrow's schedule. Cross out one item that only adds busyness, and keep the one that adds meaning.

Growth over Comfort

Would I still choose this path if it stretched me now—but built resilience for the future?

→ Comfort shelters us for today; growth equips us for tomorrow.

Action: Say yes to one thing this week that feels uncomfortable but will grow you.

Focus over Distraction

Would I still give my best energy to this if it meant ignoring the noise—but it kept me aligned with what truly matters?

→ Distraction pulls in many directions; focus moves you forward with intention.

Action: Block out one hour this week for a task that matters most—no phone, no email, no multi-tasking.

3. Mastery (Sustaining and Extending Meaning)

Living with resilience, presence, and purpose beyond recognition.

Contribution over Credit

Would I still do this if no one praised me—but it made the work or community better?

→ Praise fades quickly, but contribution leaves a lasting imprint.

Action: Do one helpful act this week that no one will know about.

Connection over Approval

Would I still reach out if they never said thank you—but our relationship grew deeper?

→ Approval is fleeting; genuine connection sustains.

Action: Reach out to one person without waiting for an occasion or thanks. Just connect.

People over Being Seen

Would I still show up if only a few people noticed—but I was fully present for the ones who mattered most?

→ Crowds may glance, but presence with a few creates memories that last.

Action: Put your phone away and give your full attention to one person who matters this week.

Purpose over Popularity

Would I still pursue this path if it never made me widely known—but it aligned deeply with my "why"?

→ Popularity drifts; purpose anchors.

Action: Write down your "why" in one sentence. Revisit it when opportunities for popularity tempt you.

THE MEANING JOURNEY MODEL RECAP

The Meaning Journey Model (figure 1) is a simple but powerful path to help shift from chasing approval to creating alignment—from performing to becoming.

MINDSET

What it means: Your internal beliefs and narratives—the lens through which you see yourself and your work.

Shift: From seeking validation to cultivating clarity

Questions:

- What beliefs are shaping how I show up?
- What stories am I still chasing?

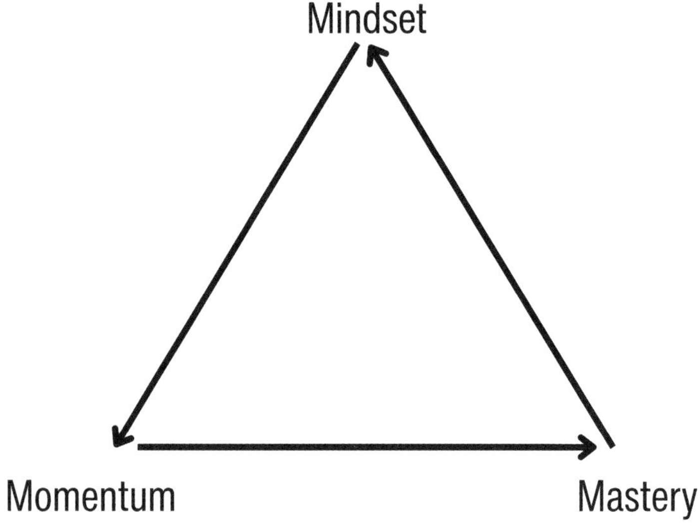

Figure 1. The Meaning Journey Model.

MOMENTUM

What it means: The intentional habits and aligned actions that keep you moving forward—not faster, but steadier

Shift: From urgency to intentional rhythm

Questions:

- What steady actions reinforce whom I want to become?
- Where am I confusing motion with meaning?

MASTERY

What it means: Quiet alignment, creating without applause, continuing despite setbacks and silence

Shift: From proving to embodying, from chasing applause to building a resilience ecosystem

Questions:

- Where am I showing up, even when no one sees?
- What helps me stay rooted in alignment under pressure?

Visual reminder:

Mindset → Momentum → Mastery

Each stage builds upon the one before it—but growth is rarely linear. Be kind to yourself in the journey. Take one aligned step at a time.

The Meaning Journey moves counterclockwise—because it's not about chasing forward to what's next but returning to what's wise and true.

THE RESOURCES

RESOURCES AND NEXT STEPS

Just as Tano's story continues beyond the page, so can yours. Your journey doesn't end with these pages—it continues through the Meaningful365 ecosystem—a movement to Work Meaningful, Live Meaningful, and Give Meaningful.

Visit **Meaningful365.com** to explore speaking engagements, workshops, and resources that help you live and lead with rhythm, not rush.

Deepen your growth through the **Meaningful365Academy.com**, offering online courses and masterclasses for individuals, teams, and employees at companies who are ready to move from inspiration to implementation.

Discover more tools and experiences—from the ***Creating Rhythm*** scroll and the **Tortoise Type™** to the **Shell Score™** and **Give Meaningful Foundation**—all designed to help you stop chasing what fades and start creating what lasts.

Meaningful365.com—The central hub for all things *meaningful*. Explore speaking inquiries, workshops, and resources designed to help teams and individuals connect purpose to performance—365 days a year—across the rhythm of Work, Live, and Give.

Meaningful365Academy.com—Deepen your growth through online courses, tip videos, and guided learning experiences designed for individuals, teams, and employees at companies who want to move from inspiration to implementation. Learn to apply the principles of alignment, rhythm, and resilience in your work and life.

WorkMeaningful.com—Bring the message to your organization through book clubs, team workshops, and leadership development experiences rooted in the *Stop Chasing, Start Creating* framework.

LiveMeaningful.com—Discover tools, challenges, and reflections that help you align your personal life with purpose and rhythm. Learn to create meaning from the inside out—one intentional day at a time.

CreatingRhythm.com—Access the full scroll of 67 wise sayings and creative reflection tools inspired by Tano's journey. This is a perfect resource for both personal and team reflection.

TortoiseType.com—Take this quick, engaging quiz to discover your unique tortoise type and what it reveals about your rhythm and growth.

ShellScore.com—Go deeper with the comprehensive, 100-question, research-backed assessment that helps you work, lead, and live with greater meaning and intentional action.

TortoisePrinciples.com—Explore the 13 Tortoise Principles that inspired this fable. Together, they form the WISEANDSTEADY™ Framework—a guide to living and leading with intention and authenticity.

GiveMeaningful.org—End where meaning begins again—with impact. The Give Meaningful Foundation builds schools, technology labs, and supports educational opportunities in under-resourced communities across Ghana and the United States. Every purchase, donation, or step you take helps students learn with dignity, teachers lead with pride, and communities thrive with hope.

Your journey doesn't end here—it grows forward.

TIPS FOR LEADERS AND TEAMS

The story you just read was written for everyone—leaders, teams, and professionals who are tired of chasing. But if you guide a team, lead an organization, or influence a group of people, you carry an extra responsibility: to shape not just your own rhythm, but the culture around you. That's why I've included this bonus toolkit. It's a set of practical ways to help your team or organization shift from chasing performance to creating meaning—while still delivering results that matter.

These aren't extra tasks to pile on top of busy schedules. They are simple practices that reshape the way you already work so that your culture reflects what matters most: alignment, rhythm, and resilience.

Use them to start conversations. Try one or two with your team. Make them your own.

The best leaders don't just run their race. They help others find their pace.

MINDSET (TEAM CULTURE)

1. Redefine Success Together

Action: Co-create a team definition of success that includes values and impact, not just output. Post it somewhere visible and revisit it quarterly.

2. Practice Story Sharing, Not Just Status Updates

Action: Open meetings with one short story about how your team's work made a difference for someone—not just progress metrics.

3. Encourage Healthy Dissent

Action: In brainstorming sessions, assign someone to respectfully challenge assumptions so that every voice is valued.

4. Model Learning Out Loud

Action: Share one thing you recently learned from failure or feedback—and invite your team to do the same.

MOMENTUM (TEAM RHYTHM AND HABITS)

5. Protect Time for Deep Work

Action: Designate one meeting-free afternoon each week where the team focuses on meaningful projects without interruption.

6. **Create Visible "Small Steps" Boards**

Action: Track not just big goals but also the small, steady progress steps the team takes. Celebrate each one publicly.

7. **Rotate Roles for Perspective**

Action: Give team members the chance to step into each other's responsibilities for a day to build empathy and appreciation.

MASTERY (SUSTAINING RESILIENCE)

8. **Recognize Resilience, Not Just Results**

Action: In reviews or team check-ins, name specific times someone persisted through challenge—even if the outcome wasn't perfect.

9. **Build Recovery into the Rhythm**

Action: Encourage team rituals of rest and reset: "no email after hours," walking meetings, or reflection rounds.

10. **Create Legacy Projects**

Action: Each quarter or annually, invite the team to choose one initiative that will leave a lasting mark—something meaningful beyond metrics.

Bonus: These practices aren't about adding more. They're about reshaping the work you already do so that it creates meaning, not just motion.

JUSTIN'S "STOP CHASING, START CREATING" KEYNOTE EXPERIENCE

A Journey through Mindset, Momentum, and Mastery to Meaning

THE FULLY IMMERSIVE, MULTISENSORY KEYNOTE-REIMAGINED EXPERIENCE

Stop Chasing, Start Creating isn't just a story—it's a framework organizations can practice. It helps teams translate Tano's journey into practical change by shifting from chasing performance to creating meaning. When individuals lead with alignment, rhythm, and resilience, workplaces don't just produce more—they thrive with purpose that lasts.

This keynote experience brings those ideas to life for your organization.

Designed for conferences, leadership summits, and company events, the keynote is a dynamic, bookable experience in which Justin guides teams through the core principles of the book in an **immersive, multisensory journey** that transforms inspiration into action. It transforms the principles of the book into an interactive, real-world experience in which participants don't just hear about meaning—they practice it.

This is not your normal keynote. It's a journey.

Rooted in the transformative power of Justin Jones-Fosu's fable ***Stop Chasing, Start Creating***, this fully immersive experience guides individuals and teams through a multisensory exploration of what it means to **lead with alignment, live with rhythm, and create with intention.**

Through storytelling, audience interaction, powerful visuals, and reflection-based prompts, participants walk Tano's journey through the Meaning Journey Model:

- **Mindset**—Recognize the internal narratives and external pressures that keep us chasing.
- **Momentum**—Build habits of meaningful action rooted in values, not vanity.
- **Mastery**—Learn to create meaning without applause—and build your resilience ecosystem.

Designed for organizations, conferences, and leadership summits that want more than a motivational message, this reimagined keynote invites people to do the deep work… beautifully.

Whether experienced in a keynote conference room, retreat, or team development session, this journey helps participants walk away with these gifts:

* A renewed sense of purpose
* Clear next steps to integrate rhythm into their work and lives
* A bold invitation to cross their own finish line—step by steady step

Optional Add-ons:

* Interactive workbook or scroll-style reflection guide
* Tortoise Type™ or Shell Score™ activation
* The Creating Rhythm Card Deck Workshop & Team Builder
* Book-signing or fireside Q&A with Justin

Learn more or bring this experience to your organization at: Meaningful365.com

THE MEANINGFUL WORK RESEARCH INITIATIVE

The ideas in *Stop Chasing, Start Creating* didn't emerge in a vacuum. They grew out of a recurring pattern Justin Jones-Fosu saw while working with leaders and teams across industries: people were working harder than ever, achieving more than ever—yet feeling increasingly disconnected from meaning in their work. That tension raised a bigger question: *Was this struggle personal—or systemic?*

To answer that question, the **Meaningful Work in America National Study** was created. Led by Justin Jones-Fosu and the Meaningful365 research team in partnership with The Center for Generational Kinetics (CGK), this nationwide research initiative examined how employees across generations and industries define, experience, and create meaningful work—and what happens when meaning is missing. Drawing insights from **750 working Americans**, the study explored the very dynamics this book brings to life:

alignment versus applause, rhythm versus rush, and resilience versus burnout.

In other words, ***Stop Chasing, Start Creating*** gives the story people feel—and the Meaningful Work in America Study provides the data that confirms it. Together, they reveal that meaningful work isn't a "nice-to-have" or a personal mindset shift alone—it's a cultural and leadership issue with measurable impact on performance, engagement, and retention.

The research uncovers the generational and organizational drivers of meaning—what truly engages people beyond pay, perks, and performance. It answers questions such as the following:

- *What makes work feel meaningful in daily life—and what gets in the way?*
- *Which leadership behaviors and cultural practices most shape meaning at work?*
- *Do younger generations expect more meaning from work than older ones ever did?*
- *Is burnout really about balance—or about a lack of meaning?*
- *Can technology and AI enhance meaning—or does it risk making work feel less human?*

This isn't just research—it's a roadmap for rethinking work.

Organizations can use these findings to spark reflection and change:

* Identify the biggest barriers keeping teams from **creating** meaning at work.
* Reimagine leadership, recognition, and purpose around what employees value most.
* Host a "Meaningful Work Conversation" using the study's key questions to bridge the gap between **purpose and performance.**

Unlike traditional engagement surveys, this study goes deeper—focusing not on how people ***feel*** about work but on how they ***create*** meaning through it. It's generational, behavioral, and actionable.

By analyzing results by generation (Gen Z to Boomers), role (leaders versus nonleaders), and work arrangement (on-site, hybrid, remote)—and much more, including how values, recognition, and belonging shape meaning across different industries and life stages—the study reveals clear, data-driven patterns leaders can act on immediately. This is not theory; it's strategy—built to help organizations connect purpose to performance and meaning to measurable impact.

When individuals connect what they do with why it matters, workplaces don't just perform better—they become places where people belong, contribute, and grow.

Explore the full study and download resources at MeaningfulWorkStudy.com.

And stay tuned for the next chapter in this movement—the global research initiative ***Meaningful Work in the World.*** Building on the US findings, this future study will explore how people across continents, cultures, generations, and industries **create** meaningful work—not by waiting for purpose to appear but by shaping it through intention, culture, and contribution. Meaningful Work in the World will reveal a new kind of result—showing how organizations unlock performance powered by purpose when their employees are empowered to create meaning where they are.

ALL ROYALTIES DONATED FOR IMPACT

All author royalties from this book are donated to the **Give Meaningful Foundation**, a nonprofit committed to advancing educational initiatives in under-resourced communities across **Ghana** and the **United States** (the author is a dual citizen of the United States and Ghana).

Your purchase helps fund:

- Clean water projects
- The construction of schools and technology labs
- Teacher support, appreciation initiatives, and meaningful projects for students

Together, we're helping students learn with dignity, teachers lead with pride, and communities thrive with hope.

Thank you for being part of something meaningful and helping the author ***"Put my money where my meaning is!"***

Learn more or get involved at: **GiveMeaningful.org**.

ACKNOWLEDGMENTS

A special thank you to my incredible wife, Tanya, for your unwavering support, thoughtful edits, and expertly timed online orders during the writing process. You carried so much behind the scenes while cheering for me at every stage—this book carries your fingerprints throughout.

I also want to thank my mother (Mom-e) for your intentionality in making sure I didn't just chase after applause but created from depth. You nurtured a mindset that helped me slow down, ask questions, and find the courage to walk steady. I would not be in a position to write this book without your beautiful, loving child-rearing (but no more washing dishes for me . . . ha!).

Thank you to Isaiah, Lydia, Peter, and David for being the best kids in the whole world. You make me a better Dad-e. You've taught me that the greatest meaning doesn't come from being seen by many but being present for a few. Thank you for challenging my ego and reminding me of what truly matters. And of course, to Chase—our energetic Labradoodle—who continues to teach me the joy of steady walks and present moments. You may not know it, but you made it into the spirit of this book too.

To the entire Meaningful365 team—thank you! You allowed me to fully focus on this project while carrying so much of the day-to-day. Your belief in this message and support in bringing it to life means the world to me. To our Ghana team … medaase. Your commitment and excellence helped make this journey possible, especially on the many writing retreats where you carried so much so that I could write.

To the Mastermind team—Stan, Marcey, Kevin, and Raven—thank you for the insight, accountability, and monthly sparks of laughter and growth. You've helped shape not just this book, but the way I show up in the world.

Steve Piersanti—my kindred brother. I could not have asked for a better editor. You believed in this project when I didn't believe in myself. You gave me hope when I had many doubts. I am so grateful we connected and were able to build this together. Let me know if you add more rules to your basketball squad because they are ingenious!

To Jeevan, thank you for your brilliant input and thought partnership in helping this book become the very best it could be. Your clarity, honesty, and insight elevated the message in powerful ways.

To the Give Meaningful Foundation and our amazing Board Members—thank you for partnering with me to create something that lasts, both in Ghana and the United States. Together, we've built our first school and tech lab—and that's just the beginning.

To the entire Berrett-Koehler publishing team—thank you for believing in this project and for being incredible partners in bringing it to the world. Your guidance, creativity, and support have made this journey not just possible, but deeply joyful.

To my AWESOME clients—from the Fortune 50 to the Fortunate Fourth Graders—you are the heartbeat behind this message. Thank you for letting me grow alongside you and for reminding me that meaningful work isn't a slogan, it's a choice.

To those who challenged me, encouraged me, and gave me space to reflect and create—thank you. Lydia and Peter, you held it down while Dad-e pulled all-nighters. I owe you a few Nerf wars.

Finally, thank YOU—the reader. For walking this journey with me. For choosing to stop chasing what fades and start creating what lasts. I hope this story gives you courage to create something meaningful in your world—step by steady step.

ABOUT THE AUTHOR

A Former Hare Who Is Learning to Walk Like a Tortoise

There was a time when Justin Jones-Fosu ran like the Hare—driven by speed, fueled by ambition, and convinced the next finish line would finally bring him peace. Every new project, every accolade, every applause felt like progress. But the faster he ran, the more he realized he wasn't racing toward meaning—he was racing past it.

So, he began to walk differently. Not slower, but steadier. He started listening more than leaping, reflecting more than reacting, creating more than chasing. In that shift, he began to discover what he now calls *meaningful work*—not work measured by applause, but by alignment; not success defined by titles, but by truth; not perfection, but purpose.

That discovery reshaped his life and his message. Today, Justin is a philanthropist, global keynote speaker, six-time award-winning author, social entrepreneur, and meaningful work researcher. He is the author of *I Respectfully Disagree: How to Have Difficult Conversations in a Divided World* and *Your WHY Matters NOW.*

As the founder of **Meaningful365**, Justin helps people and organizations lead with intention, live with meaning, and create significance through the work they do. His insights have inspired leaders across five continents, and his work has been featured in *Oprah Daily*, *TIME*, *Fast Company*, *Business Insider*, *French Business Digest*, the Associated Press, and other major outlets worldwide. He has shared his message on stages at Fortune 500 companies to grassroots leadership retreats.

But Justin's life is not defined by stages, titles, or metrics—it's shaped by a daily pursuit of purpose. His Christian faith deeply informs that pursuit, reminding him that meaning isn't something earned—it's something received and lived out through service, creativity, and generosity. He's the first to admit he doesn't always get it right. Some days faith feels clear; other days it feels messy and uncertain. Yet he keeps showing up—still learning, still growing, still choosing to begin again. That ongoing imperfection has become part of the rhythm he's learning to trust. His work is less about arriving and more about *aligning*—each day, a new chance to choose what matters most.

Justin is also the founder of the **Give Meaningful Foundation**, which directs 100% of author royalties to educational initiatives in under-resourced communities across Ghana and the United States. The foundation builds schools, funds technology labs, and supports teachers—because Justin believes meaning shouldn't stop at words; it should move through actions that change lives.

At home, Justin is a joyful husband and proud dad of four-and-a-half kids (two girls, two boys, and one energetic Labradoodle named Chase—who may soon be renamed Create). His family keeps him grounded, grateful, and laughing daily. Together, they are learning to create more than chase—and to find meaning in the ordinary moments that make life extraordinary.

Because in the end, life isn't about chasing what fades. It's about creating what lasts—step by steady step.

To connect with Justin:

- www.Meaningful365.com
- LinkedIn: Justin Jones-Fosu

Also by Justin Jones-Fosu

I Respectfully Disagree

How to Have Difficult Conversations in a Divided World

Start building bridges instead of barriers! This essential guide offers a simple 5-part framework that will help you have honest and enlightening conversations despite deep and fundamental disagreements.

We're losing the ability to disagree without dehumanizing. There is a deep need for this practical and accessible guide to having challenging conversations in any situation, from the workplace to the classroom to the dinner table.

In this book, you'll discover the 5 pillars of respectfully disagreeing: challenge your perspective, be the student, cultivate your curiosity, seek the gray, and agree to respect.

With a wide range of examples and exercises throughout, this is a timely and reader-friendly handbook to disagreeing with someone's ideology while passionately pursuing their humanity.

Berrett-Koehler
PUBLISHERS

Dear Reader,

Welcome to the Berrett-Koehler Community—a global network of changemakers creating positive impact in their lives, organizations, and communities.

Our Mission: Connecting People and Ideas to Create a World That Works for All

We believe transformation is possible. While outdated paradigms of self-interest, exclusion, and hierarchy continue to hold back our communities and organizations, we know that change can happen. That's why we connect people with actionable ideas from leading experts who are already creating the solutions we need.

The BK Way

We're an independent publisher that practices what we publish. Our books, digital resources, and community offerings provide practical pathways for building more just, equitable, and sustainable organizations and lives. Whether you're transforming your workplace, community, or personal practices, our publications meet you where you are with tools that work.

But we don't just talk about positive change—we live it. Through "The BK Way," we put stewardship and purpose before profit. As a benefit corporation, we're legally committed to benefiting all our stakeholders: authors, readers, employees, communities, and the environment.

As our gift to you, claim your free bestselling ebook at bkconnection.com/welcome. You'll also receive fresh leadership insights delivered to your inbox from bkconnection.com/blogs/the-bk-exchange.

You Make the Difference

We're grateful to our readers, authors, and community members, who bring our mission to life every day. Your stories of transformation inspire us and show others what's possible.

Share how BK publications are making a difference in your world at bkconnection.com/impact.

Your friends at Berrett-Koehler

Join the Berrett-Koehler Community

Are you passionate about supporting independent publishing and reading diverse voices and perspectives? Join the BK Community Membership Program and become a part of a vibrant literary community. To support mission-based publishing while saving up to 30 percent on all books and attending exclusive events, visit ideas.bkconnection.com/bkcommunity-join to learn more and become a member.